USING COMPUTER SCIENCE IN
FILM AND TELEVISION
≫ CAREERS ≪

XINA M. UHL

Rosen
YA
New York

Published in 2019 by The Rosen Publishing Group, Inc.
29 East 21st Street, New York, NY 10010

Library of Congress Cataloging-in-Publication Data

Names: Uhl, Xina M., author.
Title: Using computer science in film and television careers / Xina M. Uhl.
Description: First edition. | New York : Rosen YA, 2019.
| Series: Coding your passion | Includes bibliographical references and index.
Identifiers: LCCN 2018010901| ISBN 9781508183945 (library bound) | ISBN 9781508183938 (paperback)
Subjects: LCSH: Motion pictures—Vocational guidance—Juvenile literature. |
Television broadcasting–Vocational guidance—Juvenile literature. | Computer programming—Vocational guidance—Juvenile literature.
Classification: LCC PN1995.9.P75 U38 2019 | DDC 791.43029/3—dc23
LC record available at https://lccn.loc.gov/2018010901

Manufactured in the United States of America

CONTENTS

INTRODUCTION

O ne of the biggest changes in the film and television industry over the last few decades has been in the use of computers. As technology has grown both smaller and more sophisticated, it has entered ever more areas of daily life. The range of industries and applications affected by technology is astounding, including medicine, finance, government, education, banking, manufacturing, and other businesses and organizations. The entertainment industry has been greatly affected as well.

According to the ITA Media and Entertainment Top Markets Report:

> Both film and television are moving towards new digital models of consumption and distribution, and video has become a cheaper alternative to production while streaming services have overtaken traditional modes of accessing and viewing movies and television shows.

> Traditionally, the industry was made of multinational corporations, large studios, and independent studios. Increasingly, though, consumers create content on sites such as YouTube, and self-published producers are filming videos and series on low-priced digital equipment. All this has translated into one thing: jobs. The Motion Picture Association of America (MPAA) reports that it supports two million jobs in

Both software and accessories such as styluses allow users to access, edit, and manipulate film and TV shows more easily and faster than ever before.

all fifty states, resulting in $51 billion in wages. With 75 percent of film revenue coming from international markets, the entertainment industry is truly global and technology has it poised for immense growth.

The US Bureau of Labor Statistics (BLS) reports that media and communications is projected to grow 6 percent from 2016 to 2026, resulting in around forty-three thousand new jobs, with a median annual wage about 15 percent higher than all occupations. The scope of these careers is wide and varied, including jobs in movie studios, television stations and studios, and work by private vendors who provide needed sound, video, and special effects services. Many of these positions either deal with computer science and coding directly or indirectly. Coding and programming work involves a love of solving problems, openness to questioning the norm, and a willingness to be open to new ideas.

In *So, You Want to Be a Coder?* author Jane (J. M.) Bedell lists five personal traits necessary to succeed as a coder. The first is courage because coding is a trial-and-error process, and that can be frustrating. The second is creativity because solving problems can be approached from numerous—often surprising—angles, and sometimes that requires the ability to think outside the box. Logical thinking is an important skill, too, because programming runs on the assumption that there is a solution to your task, and that solution will involve breaking down the problem into smaller, more basic pieces, and then rebuilding the code to solve it. Passion carries you into the often tedious work of taking apart processes so that you can learn what you need to do to succeed. Finally, patience is a must for coders. Computer languages must be studied and practiced with persistence and dedication.

The chapters to come will provide you with valuable information about coding careers in the film and television industries. But if you are serious about getting into the entertainment industry, you will want to take the initiative by learning how to code as an individual endeavor or work with a group in clubs, camps, and other educational endeavors. Read closely to find suggestions about specific ones that suit you and your goals.

CHAPTER ONE

COMPUTER SCIENCE BASICS

B efore we get into the nitty-gritty of film and television coding jobs, let's establish some basic concepts. What exactly does computer science mean and what does it consist of? To answer these questions, it's necessary to do a little backtracking through time.

THE COMPUTER REVOLUTION

Ada Lovelace, the daughter of poet Lord Byron, kicked off the computer age way back in the early 1800s. A mathematician during a time when few women were allowed to pursue such learning, she became friends with mathematician, engineer, philosopher, and writer Charles Babbage. Babbage had designed a device called the Analytical Engine to perform complex calculations. Lovelace helped Babbage by creating a step-by-step set of instructions, or an algorithm, for it. Though the Analytical Engine never did much,

Ada Lovelace was an English translator and mathematician who was crucial in the development of algorithms.

Lovelace's efforts as the first computer programmer have gone down in the annals of history.

The next development in computer programming came during World War II at the hands of Alan Turing, the English computer scientist who created code-breaking machines. After the end of the war, he developed the Automatic Computing Engine (ACE), which could store programs in its own electronic memory. At about the same time, engineer Claude Shannon helped to develop binary programming. The most basic unit of information within a computer is called a bit, derived from the term "binary digit." Binary code consists of 1s and 0s. These bits, when arranged in patterns, instruct the computer to perform specific actions.

Early on, this code was fed into gigantic computing machines via punch cards, cards with holes punched in them to represent digital information, or by inserting and unplugging a series of wires into and out of a circuit board. Binary code was slow and unwieldy to work with and as a result, programming languages were developed to make the task easier. Programmers created common computer instructions by using words or phrases. Though this made developing programs easier, the programs did not always work perfectly and frequently needed to be fixed, or debugged.

Most early computer systems had to use customized hardware and software for their purposes. Line commands tell the computer what to do in much the same way that coding and algorithms do. By the 1980s, software company Microsoft had created an operating system to work with computer code in a more user-friendly manner. This operating system was called Windows.

As governments and businesses began to adapt to using computers, different languages developed to create programs specific to each industry. The rise of the internet in the late twentieth century accelerated the use and usefulness of computer technology. Software developers came up with web browsers, such as Microsoft's Internet Explorer, to more easily navigate the internet.

THE SPACE RACE AND THE ADVANCEMENT OF COMPUTER TECHNOLOGY

The end of World War II saw a new threat to the United States: the Soviet Union. The United States and the Soviet Union engaged in what was called the Cold War, a period of geopolitical tension during the second half of the twentieth century. As the United States promoted democracy, the Soviet Union spread Communism—two very different forms of government. In the late 1950s the Soviet Union showed its superiority in space technology by launching *Sputnik*, the first man-made object placed into Earth's orbit.

The United States was determined not to let the Soviets take first place in space, and the space race was on. The National Aeronautics and Space Administration (NASA) was created in 1958 to explore space. The race heated up over the

Virtual reality headsets actually had their beginning in 1838 with the development of the stereoscope, which used two mirrors to project one image.

years, designing, testing, and launching new space vehicles, such as the Soviet *Vostok 1* and the US Apollo program to land a man on the moon. The United States won the race when, on July 16, 1969, astronaut Neil Armstrong became the first man to walk on the moon.

To complete the moon landing, NASA engineers made significant advances in computer technology, which led to the present era of the internet, smartphones, and other digital technologies. Examples of inventions that came out of this effort are laptop computers, the joystick, 3D graphics and virtual reality, satellite navigation, water purifiers, artificial limbs, satellite television, smoke detectors, and much more.

GOING FROM MOBILE TO FILM

When cell phones were first developed, they were large and boxy and used only for communicating by voice. The world's first portable mobile phone for commercial use was the Motorola DynaTAC 8000X. It went on sale in 1983 for $4,000. As time went on and technology improved, phones became smaller, lighter, and more versatile. In 1994, the IBM Simon debuted. It was a handheld computer that utilized software applications— apps—that worked with a stylus and touch screen.

Soon after, smartphones emerged. The Blackberry devices from the early 2000s were among the first.

Today, high-quality videos can be easily shot with modern lightweight, and technically sophisticated equipment.

They made use of small keyboards. Apple's iPhone debuted in 2007, the first smartphone to use a fully functioning touch screen instead of keyboards or styluses. It also utilized text messaging and had a camera. It used an operating system called iPhone OS. This changed to iOS with the debut of the iPad tablet in 2010. Soon, competitors designed phones and devices with similar functionality, usually at a lower price. They often ran Android operating systems.

The advent of mobile devices changed the market for cameras and video cameras. Film, once the only way to capture images, has been replaced with digital technology. Since phones and digital cameras also have video recording capability, they have significantly changed the market for video cameras, including those used in the film and television industry.

CODING AND MODERN COMPUTING

Coding is the backbone of all software. It is something you don't need to wait to pursue. Google is grooming the next generation of coders through the introduction of a project called Blockly. Blockly allows young people to create computer programs by using blocks as puzzle pieces. The pieces snap together, from which users create a program without the need to type any code. Games progress in difficulty so that after each one is mastered, the student then switches to regular text-based programming.

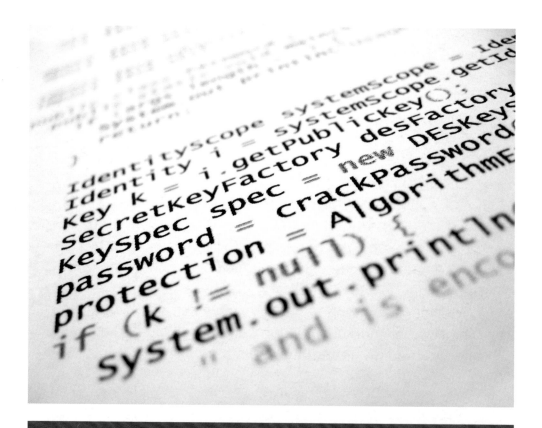

Computer code is behind the functionality of all modern computing devices, including tablets and smartphones.

Coding tools are available for the iPad through apps such as Hopscotch, Tynker, and Move the Turtle, which make learning fun. The same is true of web-based languages, such as Scratch, a visual coding system to easily make apps and games. Hackety Hack makes use of Ruby, another programming language, to teach coding to young people.

There are other coding languages and resources you can use for specific purposes:

STARTING OUT

Mark Armstrong has found success as a computer coder. When he was in elementary school, he learned the programming language BASIC and created games on his family computer. He moved onto learning Hypertext Markup Language (HTML) and PHP: Hypertext Preprocessor for developing websites. A fascination with the first iPhone led him to start a company called SavageApps. After a few years he left his company to work as a Senior iOS engineer with eBay.

When asked about what tips he had for young people interested in becoming coders, Armstrong said, as quoted in the book *So, You Want to Be a Coder?*:

Do it! Just pick a language and start playing with it. There are so many resources available for free or low cost online for those who want to learn! Take the computer science classes available to you, for sure, but don't settle for that. Play! Experiment! Explore! If you ask me, the best way to learn is by doing. Programming is one of those rare areas where given the desire, a computer, and an internet connection, you can really learn a lot.

- Python, C, C ++, and Java for general purpose coding.
- Scratch, Processing, and Maya for embedded language for video games, art, and animation

Maya is similar to the 3D animation program used by Pixar.
- Java and JavaScript for HTML/CSS (Cascading Style Sheets) for web and app development. These are markup languages that add structure, content, and style to websites.
- Arduino programming language, which is built on C++, or Lego Mindstorms NXT for robotics. They're used by the FIRST Robotics League.
- GameStar Mechanic, which is a useful platform and community to learn the principles of systems thinking and game design.

App development is increasingly used in music, sound effects, and art direction, all areas of expertise necessary in the entertainment industry. You can practice developing your own app with software development kits (SDK), online tutorials, and—the most important resource of all—the willingness to practice and make mistakes for learning's sake.

CHAPTER TWO

THE LAY OF THE ENTERTAINMENT LAND

The film and television industries have a lot in common. Both tell stories in video format and use in their production process actors, locations, sets, props, costumes, lighting, cameras, sound, special effects, and more.

Television crew members prepare for shooting a scene for a popular television series in Brooklyn, New York.

In today's interconnected world, film and television audiences span the globe. The MPAA notes, "Film and television production is an iconic American industry—and one of our country's most powerful exports. People around the world love American movies and television shows." In fact, 75 percent of theatrical revenues are generated from international audiences.

DIFFERENCES BETWEEN TELEVISION AND FILM

Though film and television have a lot in common, important differences exist between them. Television runs on more regular schedules and intense deadlines. It generally produces more content, since a series may have anywhere between eight and twenty-four half-hour to one-hour episodes. One hour of episodic television usually requires a week to film. Feature films of ninety minutes to more than two hours usually have sixty to ninety days to produce their content. It isn't unusual for films to take six to nine months to film, though. And if there are a lot of visual effects, that figure could increase.

Film often has bigger budgets than television, and more creative license in content. Films may push the envelope of storytelling and visual effects and include highly paid internationally known actors. On the other hand, television tends to be produced less extravagantly because of the tight deadlines and budget constraints. However, some television shows are shot with more attention to detail and at higher costs, such as *Game of Thrones* and *The Walking Dead*.

Television shows, depending on the network they are produced for, may have more limitations on the type of content they produce. For instance, some networks are more family friendly while others are geared more toward adults. Television also often makes use of commercial breaks several times per hour of programming since many networks are supported by advertising dollars. Films generally require an admission price at a movie theater.

While there are plenty of high-budget film productions, the growth of inexpensive digital

An actor portrays superhero Spider-Man during the shooting of the high-budget film in New York City.

equipment has encouraged zero-to-small-budget endeavors as well. YouTube has created a great platform for beginning filmmakers and series creators. Web series can be produced on websites, and are generally considerably shorter in length. Subscription channels, such as HBO and Netflix, also produce television series that may buck the trends set by other networks, in content, style, and length of series and episodes.

CHANGING TIMES

Technology has always influenced the film and television industries. These changes have risen rapidly over the last three decades. As technology continues to advance, the number of outlets for film and television production will only increase as time goes on. The advancement of broadband technology in homes and businesses allow for streaming video at rates that were previously unheard of. High-quality content continues to grow as popular outlets, such as Netflix, Hulu, and YouTube, create original series and films. Amazon, Apple, and Google are also getting involved in online streaming and original content.

What does all this mean when it comes to joining the entertainment industry? Good things. As the industry becomes ever more influenced by changing technology and channels and outlets continue to increase, so will opportunities for careers.

AMATEURS AND YOUTUBE

When most people think of YouTube, they perhaps picture funny clips of cats riding surfboards or how-to videos on everything from fixing dishwashers to learning Spanish. A lot of what is on YouTube is posted by amateurs and produced at low cost, but there are some notable exceptions.

Television programs on established networks can cost up to $5 million per episode while top-tier cable shows can cost up to $3 million per episode,

(continued on the next page)

YouTube has made it easy for anyone to distribute high-quality video, which is often shot at home without elaborate sets or expensive postproduction.

(continued from the previous page)

all this for millions of viewers. By contrast, top YouTube productions can also attract millions of viewers. However, their costs may average $30,000 to $50,000 per episode. While that is still a fair amount of money, it is a drop in the bucket compared to millions per episode. Following suit, some established network productions, such as *Awesomenesstelevision* on Nickleodeon and *Recipe Rehab* on CBS, remain online to keep production costs low. The future of film and television is likely to make further use of this cost-saving technology.

EMERGING TECHNOLOGIES

The pace of technological advances had become more rapid over the last few decades, and signs point to that trend continuing. Newly developed technologies may take a few years to hit the mainstream and bring down costs of production, but as it does so, the entertainment industry is taking more and more notice of it.

DRONES

Drones are planes without an onboard human pilot. Also called unmanned aerial vehicles or quadcopters,

It's easier than ever to fly high with lightweight, durable drones that transmit video images to cell phones or tablets.

depending on their design, drones are becoming more popular. They are starting to be used in inventive capacities in law enforcement, package delivery, military capacities, and more. They are economical sources of aerial footage for reality shows, such as *The Last Alaskans* on the Discovery Channel, or even scripted television series, such as the long-running CW show *Supernatural*.

Skills as a drone pilot can help you find jobs in film. Drones range in size from very small to larger than a full-size pickup truck. Though drones are mostly aerial, they can sometimes be used underwater. If this interests you, take classes in computer science, design, math, and engineering. Training programs are popping up at colleges and universities or at dedicated schools, such as the Unmanned Vehicle University (UVU) in Phoenix, Arizona. A solid knowledge of photography will help if your interest lies more in filming while hands-on mechanical skills can help you to design, build, and control drones. They are often controlled with software or specialized apps that need to be developed and updated.

The best place to start learning about drones is to experiment with them at home, school, or in a local club. Some drones are simple and easy to learn how to control while others are much more complicated. Familiarize yourself with the Federal Aviation Administration's (FAA) Small Unmanned Aircraft Rule, which gives guidelines for drones, such as the weight limits, hours of operation, maximum speed and altitude, and restrictions about where it is permissible to fly them. A drone pilot certification may be necessary for advanced usage.

Practice makes perfect for this skill. Often by playing with and testing out new techniques, you can become an expert like videographer Tim Sessler. He's used a drone to recreate the classic director Alfred Hitchcock's "vertigo effect" by fitting a drone with a zoom camera.

Drone photographer Will Chatham was quoted on CNBC.com as saying, "Fantastic drone footage doesn't necessarily need to be traditional aerial or 'top-down' style. Often, the best drone videos are ones that break this mold."

The film and television industry is starting to encourage inventive uses of drones through events like the New York City Drone Film Festival, which offers $5,000 each month for a director to make a film. Check out websites like AirVuz, a YouTube-like platform for videos shot by drones.

FINDING THE DRONE FOR YOU

Major uses of drones include recording aerial footage or snapping photos from unusual vantage points. If you are looking to become skilled with drone photography, consider some tips to make your learning process a little easier.

(continued on the next page)

(continued from the previous page)

Drones can vary in cost from less than $100 to in the thousands. If you're a beginner, start small with a cheaper version with less high-end photo capability. Proper equipment is a must, and proper doesn't always mean the most expensive. Read online reviews to determine the functions that are most important to you. Do you want a drone designed to work in windy conditions? How advanced should the drone's camera be? Compare flight distance and battery length as well.

Practice, practice, and then practice some more. Start with a basic drone to learn how to master the controls. If you break it, you won't be out too much money. To practice start slow and read the manual, try different maneuvers, and check out internet tutorials.

Learn how to properly configure your options and how those affect the use of the camera. Aftermarket items include gimbals (that increase shot angles), prop balancers (that even out drone flights), and first-person view (FPV) systems that stream video from your drone's camera in real time.

Finally, a preflight checklist helps you to make a habit out of ensuring that your equipment is in working order, your route is planned, the weather is acceptable, and your flight path is clear of obstacles like power lines or big trees.

CAMERAS

Camera technology has been heavily influenced by the digital revolution. Camera companies such as Arri, a German company that makes cameras for the entertainment industry, are on the cutting edge of digital usage in filming. Camera experts can use software knowledge and expertise along with mechanical know-how to perform tasks like connecting, or "slaving," cameras to one another with time codes to coordinate shooting. Obtaining an internship or experience at a company that supplies the film or television industry with equipment or services can be one way to bring you closer to your entertainment career goals.

CHAPTER THREE

THE CODE BEHIND ANIMATION

Film and television directors do a form of animation when they visualize how to shoot the video for their project. They usually create a storyboard. This refers to a process that involves laying out illustrations or images in sequence so that the writer, director, and others in the creation process can get an overall view of the story, assess timing and technical needs, and break it down into specific shots. It can resemble a comic book in format and include boxes with distinct scenes taking place in a logical order.

Storyboarding is used in a number of different capacities in various industries, including business, novel writing, theater, and more. The process was pioneered in the early twentieth century by Walt Disney Studios and originally took the form of cards or sheets of paper with sketches on them. Today in the television and film industry, it is used during preproduction, or the period of time used to organize, plan, and do other tasks necessary to getting the project started.

Digital storyboards, such as the one shown here, make it easy and cost effective to plan out shots before any filming proceeds.

Many directors use storyboarding programs and other visualization software programs. Obtaining some degree of knowledge and proficiency with these programs can make you a more attractive candidate for internships or jobs. Some of the most common are: Toon Boom's Storyboard Pro, FrameForge, StudioBinder, Moviestorm, Storyboard Quick and Storyboard Artist Studio, and Storyboard That. The downside of these programs is their high cost, with some of them topping a thousand dollars. They may be available for use at local schools, libraries, or colleges. While some of these programs provide a lower-cost monthly subscription rate, you may want to check out iOS offerings ShotPro, Storyboard Composer, or Boardo. Free options include StoryBoard Pro by Atomic Learning, Storyboard Fountain for Mac, Storyboarder, or Celtx. Bigger and fancier isn't always better, though. Storyboarding can be accomplished with index cards, paper, or using programs like Adobe Photoshop or Microsoft PowerPoint.

THE ANIMATION INDUSTRY

If there's ever an industry that tends to be on the cutting edge of computer science, it's animation. Animation refers to bringing stories to life by creating and manipulating moving images. In the early days, this meant drawing and painting images by hand on cel, or celluloid, a transparent sheet. These cels were then photographed on film. This method was time-consuming, laborious, and expensive. Modern computer-generated imagery (CGI) reduces both the time and expense needed for animation creation.

COMPUTER-GENERATED IMAGERY

One form of CGI involves the use of green screens, which have long been used in video production, usually to isolate a human figure from their background in order to insert computer-generated settings, creatures, or images into the film. Called

The detail and sophistication of computer-generated imagery, such as the scene here, continue to develop, making it difficult to distinguish it from traditional photography.

chroma key, green-screen technology has numerous uses including depicting figures in outer space, for example. One of the most familiar uses of green-screen technology occurs on the weather forecasts during the nightly news broadcast. Computerized images of storm cells and heat waves are generated to run behind or beside news anchors, who point to various elements of the animation.

Pure animation refers to cartoons, which feature living creatures that are approximations of themselves. They are 2D, or two dimensional; not designed to exist in the real world. A step up in animation is 3D computer graphics. It makes use of motion-capture technology to portray characters with excellent realism and human- or animal-like characteristics similar to those in the real world. Though, like Gollum in *The Lord of the Rings* films or Caesar, the ape in *The Planet of the Apes* films, these beings could not exist outside the realm of cinema.

Motion-capture technology allows computers to mimic the movements and expressions of living beings.

The most common methods of achieving motion-capture are optical-passive or optical-active.

Optical-passive motion-capture involves having an actor wear reflective markers on certain body parts. These markers are tracked by two to fifty, or more, infrared cameras. They track the actor's coordinates as data, which can then be applied to CGI characters. This has the effect of making their movements more realistic. Optical-active capture involves an actor wearing a suit fitted with LED markers. They generate their own light instead of reflecting it back for the cameras.

Facial performance capture is a specific form of motion capture. Facial expressions involve subtle and minute muscle movements, which people are highly attuned to recognize. This is why many animated video games or movies include characters whose expressions are not quite right when compared to real life.

Computer science is so intimately connected with these animation efforts that the next step is to create completely virtual actors who respond only to computer-guided clues. Production studios will no doubt be on the cutting edge of such new technology.

While general animation skills are helpful, sometimes employees of animation studios or private vendor companies that work for studios may specialize in the creation of certain characters, actions, or backgrounds and settings.

THE ART OF CODING

Danielle Feinberg is the director of photography for lighting at Pixar. She's worked on many popular animated movies including *Brave, WALL-E, Monsters, Inc., A Bug's Life,* and *Finding Nemo*. She describes her job in the book *So, You Want to Be a Coder?*:

> We build this three-dimensional world inside the computer and we have icons that represent lights that I move around in the world. So if it's sunset, I add a light that's the sun and put it near the horizon and color it orange and get nice purple-blue light bouncing down from the sky. And I have control over the shadow, the color, the atmosphere, the quality of the light.

Feinberg's job involves working with special software and writing code to make daily tasks easier or to create a new effect entirely. She describes writing code as "very much a creative process." It's not always easy, though. Bugs in the code can make for long hours of experimentation and searching for answers. She doesn't seem to mind, though.

Feinberg got started way back in fourth grade when she took her first coding class. As a member of an artistic family, she took art classes while young, and later leveraged this experience to gain a position at one of the most high-profile animation studios in the world.

This shot from Disney's *Finding Nemo* demonstrates the attention to detail and visual impact possible by the use of sophisticated code in modern animation.

JOB CATEGORIES IN ANIMATION

In general, skills that are necessary for animation work are biomechanics, engineering, and motion capture. Compatible college majors include computer science and computer animation. Advanced computer skills and math go hand-in-hand. Creativity and art courses provide you with an understanding of light, color, and texture. A willingness to experiment and exercise creativity will help you combine your skills. Familiarity with animation software packages is key. Six of the most popular are Toon Boom Studio 8 (mainly for 2D animation), Blender, Autodesk's 3Dds Max (Mari for 3D animation skills), Unity Pro 4 for game creation, and Adobe Photoshop CS6 in order to edit photos and create original images. Many of these programs may be available for use through a school, university, library, or other educational institution. Blender is free and open source, so it is a good program to start with.

Some of the biggest, best-known companies that specialize in animation hire for a range of positions. Industrial Light and Magic employs technical animators and DreamWorks hires motion capture engineers. Skills and an educational background in media arts, graphic design, and computer science, are good supplements to courses in motion capture and animation.

It's always worthwhile to apply for summer internships at companies such as DreamWorks and Pixar Animation. Keep in mind that these internships are highly competitive, so the more skills you have, the better. Attendance at a local computer coding camp can help you gain knowledge and provide you with opportunities to get to know presenters and program directors.

Getting to know fellow participants can help as well, since jobs in the entertainment industry often do not involve the placement of job positions at recognized job websites or in employment publications. Word-of-mouth and recommendations from current staff members usually carry a lot of weight during the hiring process.

CHAPTER FOUR

POSTPRODUCTION TECH

A lot of the work involving computer science in the entertainment industry takes place after the initial filming is done. This stage of work is referred to as postproduction, and it involves the use of talented coders to create, modify, and update programs that enhance or add to the appearance of already filmed material. You can get a head start on your career no matter what stage you are in by familiarizing yourself with programs used in the industry.

WORKING WITH HIGH-END SOFTWARE TOOLS

One of the best-known high-end software programs and tools for editing, color manipulation, and audio is put out by Blackmagicdesign and is called DaVinci Resolve 14. Professional consoles provide a number of configurations for different levels of productions, from

Postproduction computer consoles provide a variety of settings and options depending upon the project's needs.

simple to complex. DaVinci Resolve 14 is available on Mac, Windows, and Linux platforms as a free download or a paid multiuser studio version. This tool is frequently used in films and television and includes sophisticated editing tools to edit, mix, and master sound; to identify faces or even out tones, brighten eyes, and other color corrections. It includes multicamera editing, transitions, and high-velocity shots.

Pro Tools is put out by Avid Technology and includes hardware and software for professional music and audio production. Called a digital audio workstation it can function as software alone or to operate a number

Professional audio mixing boards may look intimidating, but once you pick up the fundamentals of operation, you will appreciate the range of options available to you.

of different converters and processors. It acts like an audio mixer and multitrack tape recorder.

One job that utilizes experience with Pro Tools is postproduction sound intern with Sony Pictures Entertainment in the Los Angeles area. The position involves working in all stages of post sound production in both television and feature film; learning to rerecord actors' dialogue, use sound design, Foley editorial, and dialogue processes, and programs from industry professionals; and receiving mentoring from management regarding goals and career paths. Qualifications include prior college sound editing projects and classes and the ability to run and use Pro Tools technology. Internships, which are often seasonal, are highly desirable because they are designed to be entry level but also to provide you with mentors and real-world experience.

The Dolby Institute is a powerhouse in audio production. They offer a number of tools for the entertainment industry such as Dolby Atmos and Dolby Surround 7.1. High definition (HD) and 3D tools are developed under the Dolby brand as well.

The Adobe suite of products is widely used as well. This includes Adobe After Effects, which is used to

Postproduction utilizes Adobe After Effects for motion graphics, visual effects, editing audio, and more.

create movie titles, intros, or add elements such as fire, rain, and fog. Videos or images can be combined, colors manipulated, and animation added. It works well with another Adobe product that is used widely in the industry—Photoshop. Both programs are available with special monthly rates and discounts for students, though you may find them at your local school or library as well.

Technicolor products are used for credits as well as visual effects, color finishing, sound, and animation.

HOUR OF CODE

Every year, the Hour of Code takes place during Computer Science Education Week in early December. The event is designed to provide an introduction to computer science that lasts just one hour. The idea is to show that anyone can learn the basics.

The event has reached millions of students in more than 180 countries speaking over forty-five languages. There's no age restriction either. In one recent year, more than 150,000 Hour of Code events occurred worldwide.

In the fall, start looking for an Hour of Code event near you through their website, or start one yourself or through your school. Guidelines, instructions, and tutorials are available online.

3D PRINTING IN FILM

Once upon a time, 3D printers were the stuff of dreams. And when the first ones were developed, their price tags were astronomical. But as 3D technology matured and became more widespread, prices dropped and more uses became apparent in the business world. The printer does not just create a 2D object like a piece of paper with text or images on it. Instead, it uses a computer-aided-design (CAD) file, which specifies the width, height, length, and special features of an object such as a figurine or tool. The printer utilizes material such as plastic to build the object layer by layer. In order to get the specifications, or specs, for building a model from an existing item, designers make use of 3D scanners to obtain its measurements.

The ability to make such objects means that prototypes or models of bigger objects can be made first. One example of this is the suit worn by actor Robert Downey Jr. in *Iron Man 2*. Designers were able to create a small version of the suit to give to the director and producers for their feedback. They could then make alterations before creating the life-size version. A similar approach was taken for the Demogorgon monster in the series *Stranger Things*.

Stop-motion animated films such as *Coraline, The Boxtrolls*, and *ParaNorman* make use of 3D printers to create different facial expressions for the puppets that serve as the characters. Recently, a pioneer in this field, Laika, a company based in Portland, Oregon, won the Academy of Motion Picture Arts and

Sciences' Scientific and Engineering Award for their achievements using such technology.

If working with 3D printing interests you, learn to use CAD software either on your own or by taking classes in it. Then experiment on 3D printers in your

In the movie *The Hunger Games: Mockingjay Part 2*, stars Jennifer Lawrence, Liam Hemsworth, Natalie Dormer, and others gather around a hologram of a city, made with CGI effects.

school or in another public venue such as your local library.

ENTERING THE FIELD OF VISUAL EFFECTS

"Visual effects" refers to digital elements added to video such as explosions, floods, scenery, and backgrounds. It can recreate thousands of warriors on

a battlefield, or it can involve deleting images from a scene, like a building from a scene's background.

One career in this field is visual effects artist, also known as an inferno artist, or multimedia artist. This person specializes in CGI effects that might be too dangerous, costly, or impossible to film otherwise. Areas of education to focus on are science—physics in particular—math, computer science, and art and design. Some universities offer courses in computer animation and visual effects, though a degree in computer science is good as well. Gathering a portfolio of work to show potential employers is a smart move.

Another career is FX technical director. This individual creates simulations of fluids, cloth, hair, and digital effects like smoke, fire, clouds, water, steam, and explosions. These effects are added after shooting with software such as Houdini, Maya, and in-house programs. Requirements include skills in math, science, engineering, and, of course, computers. This position is a blend of technical skill with creativity. Pertinent college majors are computer science and computer animation.

CHAPTER FIVE

PROMOTION, SECURITY, AND BUDGETS

Computer careers exist in areas other than production of video and the effects and sound that go along with it. A recent Top Markets Report for Media and Entertainment said that the US "market represents a third of the global industry." With such a large share of the industry, publicity and promotion are vital parts of drawing viewers to television shows, networks, and motion pictures.

The internet is a significant source of promotion, particularly websites that feature trailers and clips of upcoming shows and films. Interviews with actors are popular, as are forums that provide viewers with places for reviews, games, and other special features designed to promote content. In order to pursue a career that involves all or some of these venues, you will want to learn HTML and CSS to design websites and control the look and functionality of websites.

By familiarizing yourself with HTML and CSS, you will find it possible to write computer code to adjust web graphics with ease.

LEARNING WEB DEVELOPMENT

An example of a real-world job is that of a web developer. In addition to being responsible for the look of a website, they also manage the site's performance. Some provide content for the site. If you possess graphic design skills along with a talent for understanding technology, this may be the path for you.

The current BLS's *Occupational Outlook Handbook* reports that around 17 percent of web developers worked in computer systems design and related industries just a couple of years ago. Roughly the same percentage of workers were self-employed. This position generally requires knowledge of and skills with HTML, CSS, and Adobe Photoshop. Familiarity with Flash FTP, a file transfer protocol client software, and Microsoft Project, software designed to manage complicated projects and teams, is desirable. Educational requirements are flexible.

While a college degree in computer science may be necessary for a position in private industry, a high school diploma and self-taught skills may be all you need for some jobs or to start your own web development business.

According to the BLS, the job outlook is strong, projected to grow 15 percent in the decade up to 2026. Demand for this career is tied to the increasing popularity of e-commerce and mobile devices.

GAME DEVELOPMENT

The immense popularity of video games has not gone unnoticed by the entertainment industry. An article on Nasdaq.com reported that in 2015 the gaming industry began to pull in more revenue than movies and music, a 5 percent jump in one year. This trend is only expected to increase in the years to come. By 2022, the industry is predicted to bring in $230 billion per year, according to a report by game-industry advisors Digi-Capital.

Development of computer games continues at a frantic pace due to its popularity and profitability. This developer is creating a game for the company Gameloft.

The role of games will likely increase in film and television, too. Games will either function as a means of promoting new releases (or in some cases the game may spawn the development of movies itself) or in applications that appear in the shows themselves. While the latter use of games is still in development, it may appear soon on the horizon of the entertainment industry. To prepare for a career in gaming, study computer game design, computer science, and graphic design. Teamwork is important in this industry, so learning to work effectively in a team is more than a nice skill to have—it can mean the difference between keeping a job and losing it.

An example of job qualifications for an entry-level game programmer include good communication skills; two or more years of experience with C/C++; and at least one year of experience with scripting languages such as Perl, Lua, and C#. Preferred skills include being an avid video game enthusiast and knowledge of Microsoft Excel, a spreadsheet program with the ability to make both simple and complex calculations.

CREATE A VIDEO GAME AT CAMP

For two decades, iD Tech has been committed to providing summer tech camps for young people. Video game design and development camps are among the most popular programs they offer. At the time of this writing, camps were located in twenty-nine states (including both northern and southern California locations) and internationally in Hong Kong, Singapore, and the United Kingdom. The company also offers other tech camps such as coding, design, and robotics, all geared for young people aged seven through eighteen.

If you don't think iD Tech is an option for you, check out the YMCA, which offers summer technology camps at many of its 2,700 locations in the United States alone.

CYBERSECURITY AND PROTECTION

Cybersecurity is a concern when building websites, offering content digitally, and just doing business in general with the help of computers. Cyberattacks involve an unauthorized intrusion from one computer to another or to a website. The goal of these attacks are to gain sensitive information such as bank account numbers or passwords. Attackers use this data to commit fraud, release movies or television shows illegally, or change a website's content.

Author Jane (J. M.) Bedell lists a number of cyberattacks in her book *So, You Want to Be a Coder?* They include:

- **Brute-Force Attacks.** These attacks are designed to try numerous combinations of letters, numbers, and symbols in an effort to access your passwords. A dictionary attack uses word combinations to locate passwords; this led to the inclusion of symbols and numbers in passwords. Phishing is malicious links in emails that are designed to misdirect the user to fake websites with the goal of stealing valuable information and passwords.
- **Denial-of-Service Attacks.** This type of attack overloads a website with either traffic or data until it no longer displays the right pages and becomes more vulnerable to hackers finding their way into your systems.
- **Malware.** This computer code is designed to steal private information or destroy content on

Cyberattacks are an unfortunate fact of life for governments, businesses, and individuals.

computers. Spyware is a type of malware that collects keystroke data from infected computers and steals private information like passwords.

- **Viruses.** These specially written computer codes hide on your device and replicate themselves, causing system malfunctions and data corruption. They can be attached to files you download from the internet. Worms can replicate themselves like viruses, but they do not attach to files or programs. Instead they survive on their own and become more dangerous than viruses. Ransomware is a form of malicious software designed to hold your data hostage until a fee, or ransom, is paid.

While computers are protected from malware by firewalls and encryption codes, among other things, new forms of security attacks are invented frequently, making it necessary to keep on top of the latest

THE COST OF PIRACY

It made big news. Season seven of *Game of Thrones* was pirated more than a billion times worldwide. This number exceeded the number of paying viewers by more than tenfold. The season seven finale racked up more than 120 million pirated copies within just three days of its premiere.

Digital TV Research estimated that such piracy cost American companies more than $30 billion in lost sales. This number is projected to increase to more than $50 billion by 2022. Pirated movies and television shows are most often found on websites that host uploaded movies and television episodes. Typically, such websites operate outside the United States. The sheer scale of these numbers makes it clear that piracy is an issue that entertainment professionals need to take seriously. This will translate into more attention paid to cybersecurity—and more job openings in the field.

developments in the field. TechRepublic reports that cybersecurity job roles are hard to fill with qualified candidates. Skilled personnel can command salaries in excess of $100,000 per year, making this an attractive job choice. Degrees in either computer science or math are helpful, as is knowledge of Python and Java.

THE ALL-IMPORTANT BUDGET

President Harry S. Truman is famous for saying, "The buck stops here," referring to the final authority of the president's office. However, in the entertainment industry—and business in general—if the bucks stop, so does everything else. Money is the bottom line, and as such, a lot of careers are available to manage, assess, and analyze that money.

Perhaps you never considered finance, math, and accounting jobs as ways to use your skills and talents in the entertainment industry. You should, because these fields all utilize computer science to a great degree. In addition, the number of jobs available are high, and by getting in the door at a large movie studio, for example, you can take advantage of opportunities to change jobs within the company to get something closer to what you might want.

Computer usage and skills are necessary if you are looking for an office job in the entertainment industry. Programming skills are much less important than a good working knowledge of office software such as Microsoft's Excel, Word, PowerPoint, and

Outlook. Examples of job responsibilities in offices involve managing executives' calendars, preparing presentations for meetings, writing letters and reports, and calculating budgets.

If you have a talent and passion for math, you will find that you are in a good position for many jobs in the entertainment industry. Math is used for a number of functions such as tracking sales of opening weekend movie tickets, assessing budgets, making sure invoices are paid for vendors and equipment, predicting future trends and revenue, and more.

Looking for entry-level assistant, executive assistant, or analyst positions can be a good

Spreadsheets are used in most businesses, including film and television. Becoming familiar with the use of spreadsheets can make you a valuable asset in the office.

strategy. Generally, these jobs require attention to detail, organizational abilities, strong analytical skills, and proficiency with the Microsoft suite of programs. An enduring excitement for television and movies is a quality often not appreciated as necessary by applicants such as yourself. But there's a good chance that the managers and administrators who are doing the hiring share your same enthusiasm, and this shared interest can make you a more attractive candidate. Once you get your foot in the door, you can look for opportunities to move up the company ladder into a more advanced position or into a different department.

An example of an office job in administration is that of a production financial analyst for Walt Disney. This particular position requires knowledge of math, computer software packages, the entertainment industry, and analytical and math skills. Appropriate college majors are accounting, finance, and mathematics.

CHAPTER SIX

VIRTUAL REALITY, ARTIFICIAL INTELLIGENCE, AND THE FUTURE OF ROBOTICS

While summer moviegoers are watching the latest blockbuster, they may notice some changes in the theater. Technologies that enhance the moviegoing experience are currently being rolled out in limited fashion. Theater chairs may shake to simulate airplane turbulence, for instance. Jets of air may blow over the audience to simulate wind. Water may even fall from above to simulate the rainy scenes on screen.

Virtual reality (VR) may soon raise the entertainment experience to new levels. Virtual reality refers to technology that allows users to become completely immersed in an environment generated by computer—360 degrees of 3D video. Users can move and hear sounds in this virtual environment. Special VR headsets are necessary for the experience. Examples of these headsets are those connected to gaming consoles such as PlayStation VR; Oculus Rift, which is connected to a computer; and stand-alone

Oculus Rift makes use of a VR headset to immerse the user in a computer-generated environment. It can be used for gaming, simulating a viewer's cinema experience, education, and more.

devices such as Google Cardboard. They often work in combination with a smartphone.

Statista reports that the market in VR is going one place: up. Just a couple of years ago, this market brought in $3.7 billion worldwide and it should skyrocket to $40.4 billion in the next couple years. This phenomenal growth points out how VR will be the next big thing in moviegoing—if not, the entertainment industry risks being left behind the technological curve.

Virtual reality will change the moviegoing experience not just through the gear necessary to experience it, but also because the viewer will become an active participant in the story, able to choose the story's direction in much the same way that video gamers can direct the course that their games take.

Sony Pictures offers a Virtual Reality Intern summer position for their motion picture group. It involves learning how to operate, maintain, and demonstrate high-end VR platforms; review current products for feedback; keep abreast of new content and developments; and help establish a strategy for the company to make use of this emerging technology. Qualifications include coursework and experience in VR and knowledge of and interest in emerging media technologies.

RIGHT PLACE, RIGHT TIME

There are certain places where the film and television industry is primarily located, and if you are serious about a career in it, it's good to be in the center of the action. The granddaddy of locations is Los Angeles, California, especially a neighborhood in the middle of the city called Hollywood. While other centers of film and television production are growing in importance—such as Atlanta, Toronto, and Vancouver—Los Angeles is still the most common place to find movie and television studios, and the businesses that contract with them such as special effects and visual effects firms, audio specialists, and other vendors.

While it is always a good idea to apply for advertised job openings at your chosen place of employment, don't let that be the only action you take to find work. Post your résumé on the professional social network LinkedIn, join specialty groups such as your alumni association or networking organizations, and sign up for work at temporary "temp" agencies. Large and small employers alike make use of temp agencies to fill vacancies. The advantage for employees is that you can find yourself assigned to film studios or associated businesses. Since the positions are temporary, you are free to try out work in different departments to see how you like it—and how they like you. If there's a good fit, many times you will be offered a full-time position. But it all starts with putting yourself out there where the jobs are.

LinkedIn can provide you with valuable contacts to pursue your dream job. Participate in one of the many groups available to learn, view job openings, and network effectively.

ARTIFICIAL INTELLIGENCE

A developing field that utilizes computer science in the entertainment world is that of algorithms for making recommendations and determining the popularity of films and television shows. Algorithms have been used for some time at Amazon.com to provide recommendations of other products users might be interested in. For instance, if you purchase a book on how to learn the Python computer language, the algorithm will use a calculation to flag other, similar book titles and show them on certain Amazon pages with the goal of selling you more products.

Such algorithms are a form of AI, and they are hotter than hot as large streaming content providers struggle to get and keep consumers' business. They are designed to get the right content to the person who would most appreciate it.

Netflix uses a similar process to recommend titles for you to watch based on what you have previously watched and/or rated as an area of interest.

Netflix currently has over a hundred million streaming subscribers worldwide. As the strength of its user base grows, Netflix continually searches for new and better ways to promote their original series and other programs. The recommendations are one way to solve what is called the "rabbit hole problem," which refers to so much available content that users have no way to filter through it. Netflix's Chris Jaffe, vice president of product innovation, described the

Companies such as Netflix use sophisticated algorithms and artificial intelligence to recommend shows and movies based on the user's past viewing preferences.

idea behind recommendation algorithms to *Business Insider*:

> We don't really care if you watch *Jessica Jones* or *Marco Polo,* we just want you to watch. We have to make customers happy and that's the single guiding light. As we think about customers, we think about how they are spending their time. The biggest challenge for Netflix is: if you're tired and it's the end of the day, you could read a book or a magazine, you could go on Facebook, watch linear

television, or watch Netflix. We want to make Netflix so engaging you keep choosing it.

Such algorithms are imprecise gauges of human preference. If they weren't, every television show would be wildly popular. But they represent an enticing field of study for those who excel in mathematics, statistics, and computer science.

If you are interested in learning more, you will want to check out an open-source AI framework released by Amazon.com called Deep Scalabale Sparse Tensor Network Engine, or DSSTNE. Pronounced "destiny," DSSTNE is part of a number of AI projects called deep learning used by large, innovative companies such as Google, Amazon, and others. As reported on Github, Amazon released this network engine:

So that the promise of deep learning can extend beyond speech and language understanding and object recognition to other areas such as search and recommendations. We hope that researchers around the world can collaborate to improve it. But more importantly, we hope that it spurs innovation in many more areas.

By familiarizing yourself with this software and others that are similar, you will be on the cutting edge of the future in the entertainment industry.

ROBOTS

The building and use of robots in entertainment is also an effort poised to grow over the next decades.

Robots are in use as animatronic figures, which function like motorized puppets. They are controlled remotely and utilize sophisticated software. It is tricky for designers to create animatronic figures that move like living creatures, but developments are underway. The mathematics of movement is an open field for software developers of the future.

RoboScreens is an example of an up-and-coming development in robotics. It refers to a screen mounted to a robot arm that uses specially developed software to control movement. It makes use of Maya 3D graphics software to create interactive visual effects in both film and video games.

The robotics industry is predicted to total $67 billion by 2025 as technology gets cheaper and more efficient. Part of those billions will be spent in the entertainment industry in as-yet-undreamed-of applications.

GLOSSARY

algorithm A set of steps to complete a computer process.

amateur A person who lacks experience or skill in an art or science.

bit A unit of computer information that is expressed as a 0 or 1.

celluloid Film used to make movies.

circuit board Many electrical circuits attached to a board.

commands An written instruction that directs the computer to take a certain action.

Communism A society in which the government owns the things that make and transport products, and private property does not exist.

debug To fix problems in the functioning of computer programs.

drone An unmanned flying craft controlled by a computer or person on the ground.

green screen When a single color such as green is used as a backdrop in filming to make it easy for background images to be added easily.

hardware The physical components of a computer.

mentor To teach or provide guidance to someone.

motion-capture The process of using a device to capture live movements.

operating system Software that allows a user to access a computer's basic functions.

preproduction Work done in preparation of filming a program.

production The process of filming a television or cinematic program.

postproduction Work done to correct or enhance a filmed program.

quadcopter An unmanned aircraft with four rotors.

script The written text of a television or cinematic program.

software Programs that direct a computer to perform certain functions.

stop-motion A filming technique involving objects like clay models placed in positions that mimic movement.

storyboard A set of images arranged consecutively to show the actions in a movie or television show.

stylus A penlike device to enter data into a computer.

The Association for Unmanned Vehicle Systems International (AUVSI)
2700 South Quincy Street, Suite 400
Arlington, VA 22206
(703) 845-9671
Website: http://www.auvsi.org
Facebook: @AUVSI-316376653645
Twitter and Instagram: @auvsi
The association provides industry news, events, and networking through their website and membership in the world's largest unmanned systems community.

Canada's Association of Information Technology Professionals (CIPS) National Office
1375 Southdown Road, Unit 16, Suite 802
Mississauga, Ontario L5J 2Z1
Canada
(905) 602-1370
(877)-ASK-CIPS (275-2477)
Website: http://www.cips.ca
Facebook: CIPS.ca
CIPS offers networking opportunities, certification of information technology professionals, accreditation of IT university and college programs, and an IT job board.

Code.org
1501 4th Avenue, Suite 900
Seattle, WA 98101

Website: https://code.org
Facebook: @Code.org
Twitter and Instagram: @codeorg
A nonprofit organization, Code.org is dedicated
    to "expanding access to computer science in
    schools and increasing participation by women and
    underrepresented minorities." They offer a number
    of coding courses for grades K–12 and beyond, and
    sponsor the Hour of Code event.

Digital Media Academy
105 Cooper Court
Los Gatos, CA 95032
(866) 656-3342
Website: https://www.digitalmediaacademy.org
Facebook: @digitalmediaacademy.org
Twitter: @DMA_org
Instagram: @digitalmediaacademy
The academy provides summer camps and online
    tutoring in coding, game design, filmmaking,
    photography, 3D modeling, and robotics across the
    country and in Canada.

Get In Media
3300 University Boulevard
Winter Park, FL 32792
(407) 772-8549
Website: http://getinmedia.com
Twitter: @getinmedia
GetInMedia.com offers company profiles, job
    descriptions, and the inside scoop from media
    professionals about the entertainment business.

It charts the media landscape and provides news, interviews, and features about people in the industry.

Motion Picture Association of America (MPAA)
1301 K Street NW, Suite 900E
Washington, DC 20005
(202) 293-1966
Email: contactus@mpaa.org
Website: https://www.mpaa.org
Facebook: @MotionPictureAssociationAmerica
Twitter: @MPAA
The mouthpiece for the motion picture, home video, and television industry in America, the association is a source for career information, news, film ratings, and more.

FOR FURTHER READING

Bedell, Jane (J. M.). *So, You Want to Be a Coder?* New York, NY: Simon & Schuster, 2016.

Centore, Michael. *Entertainment Industry*. Broomhill, PA: Mason Crest, 2017.

Gregory, Josh. *Apps: From Concept to Consumer*. New York, NY: Scholastic, Inc., 2015.

Kassnoff, David. *What Degree Do I Need to Pursue a Career in Information Technology & Information Systems?* New York, NY: Rosen Publishing, 2015.

Mara, Wil. *Software Development*. New York, NY: Scholastic, Inc., 2016.

McKinney, Devon. *A Day at Work with a Software Developer*. New York, NY: PowerKids Press, Rosen Publishing, 2016.

Mooney, Carla. *STEM Jobs in Movies*. Vero Beach, FL: Rourke Educational Media, 2015.

Rauf, Don. *Virtual Reality.* New York, NY: Rosen Publishing, 2016.

Saujani, Reshma. *Girls Who Code: Learn to Code and Change the World.* New York, NY: Viking, Penguin Young Readers Group, 2017.

Uhl, Xina M. *Strengthening Collaborative Project Skills*. New York, NY: Rosen Publishing, 2018.

Aggarwal, Neeraj, Frank Arthofer, Fredrik Lind, John
Rose, Jacob Rosenzweig, and Joachim Stephan.
"The Digital Revolution Is Disrupting the Television
Industry." BCG, March 21, 2016. https://www
.bcg.com/publications/2016/media-entertainment
-digital-revolution-disrupting-tv-industry.aspx.

Andrews, Travis M. "'Game of Thrones' Was Pirated
More Than a Billion Times — Far More Than It Was
Watched Legally." *Washington Post*, September 8,
2017. https://www.washingtonpost.com/news
/morning-mix/wp/2017/09/08/game-of-thrones
-was-pirated-more-than-a-billion-times-far-more-than
-it-was-watched-legally/?utm_term=.1c2262d6f9bc.

Bedell, Jane (J. M.). *So, You Want to Be a Coder?* New
York, NY: Simon & Schuster, 2016.

Bureau of Labor Statistics, U.S. Department of
Labor. "Media and Communication Occupations."
Occupational Outlook Handbook, January 30, 2018.
https://www.bls.gov/ooh/media-and
-communication/home.htm.

Bureau of Labor Statistics, U.S. Department of Labor.
"Multimedia Artists and Animators." *Occupational
Outlook Handbook*. Retrieved on February 27,
2018. https://www.bls.gov/ooh/arts-and-design
/multimedia-artists-and-animators.htm.

Bureau of Labor Statistics, U.S. Department of Labor.
"Web Developers." *Occupational Outlook Handbook*.
Retrieved on February 28, 2018. https://www.bls
.gov/ooh/computer-and-information-technology
/web-developers.htm.

Computer Hope. "Computer vs. Smartphone." January 24, 2018. https://www.computerhope.com/issues/ch001398.htm.

Danesh, Darya. "Top 11 Storyboard Software of 2018 (with free Storyboard Templates)." Studiobinder. https://www.studiobinder.com/blog/top-10-storyboard-software-of-2016-free-storyboard-templates.

Design World. "Entertainment Application May Change Robot Control and Programming." March 5, 2013. https://www.designworldonline.com/entertainment-application-may-change-robot-control-and-programming.

Digi-Capital. "Games Software/Hardware $165B+ in 2018, $230B+ in 5 Years, Record $2B+ Investment Last Year." January 2018. http://www.digi-capital.com/news/2018/01/games-software-hardware-165b-in-2018-230b-in-5-years-record-2b-investment-last-year/#.Wpb2iujwaM_.

Federal Aviation Administration. "Summary of Small Unmanned Aircraft Rule (Part 107)." June 21, 2016. https://www.faa.gov/uas/media/Part_107_Summary.pdf.

Finley, Klint. "Amazon's Giving Away the AI Behind Its Product Recommendations." *Wired*, May 16, 2016. https://www.wired.com/2016/05/amazons-giving-away-ai-behind-product-recommendations.

Forbes. "The Difference between Virtual Reality, Augmented Reality and Mixed Reality." February 2, 2018. https://www.forbes.com/sites/quora/2018/02/02/the-difference-between

-virtual-reality-augmented-reality-and-mixed
-reality/#7aed54712d07.

Github.com. "Amazon DSSTNE: Q&A." September 30,
2016. https://github.com/amzn/amazon-dsstne
/blob/master/FAQ.md.

Hedstrom, Jess. "3D Printing is Revolutionizing the
Entertainment Industry." Sculpteo, February 24,
2016. https://www.sculpteo.com
/blog/2016/02/24/3d-printing-is-revolutionizing
-the-entertainment-industry.

History.com Staff. "The Space Race." A+E Networks,
2010. http://www.history.com/topics/space-race.

Juang, Mike. "Drone Entrepreneurs Take Flight as
Costs Fall and Money-Making Rises." CNBC, June
17, 2017. https://www.cnbc.com/2017/06/17/3
-ways-you-can-turn-flying-drones-into-a-money-making
-job.html.

Kelly, Tiffany. "The Booming Demand for Commercial
Drone Pilots." *The Atlantic,* January 30, 2017.
https://www.theatlantic.com/technology
/archive/2017/01/drone-pilot-school/515022.

Kolbe, Kerry. "Space Race Legacy: 10 Technologies
Still in Use Today." *Telegraph*, February 9, 2017.
http://www.telegraph.co.uk/films/hidden-figures
/technology-from-the-space-race.

Mead, Rob. "10 Tech Breakthroughs to Thank the
Space Race For." Techradar.com, July 20, 2009.
http://www.techradar.com/news/world-of-tech
/10-tech-breakthroughs-to-thank-the
-space-race-for-617847.

Motion Picture Association of America. "Driving
Economic Growth." Retrieved February 6, 2018.

https://www.mpaa.org/what-we-do/driving
-economic-growth.

Nath, Trevir. "Investing in Video Games: This Industry Pulls in More Revenue Than Movies, Music." Nasdaq, June 13, 2016. https://www.nasdaq.com /article/investing-in-video-games-this-industry-pulls -in-more-revenue-than-movies-music-cm634585.

Nations, Daniel. "A List of iPad Models and Generations." Lifewire, February 1, 2018. https:// www.lifewire.com/list-of-ipad-models-and -generations-1994232.

Nations, Daniel. "What Is the iPhone OS (iOS)?" Lifewire, August 25, 2017. https://www.lifewire .com/what-is-ios-1994355.

O'Reilly, Lara. "Netflix Lifted the Lid on How the Algorithm That Recommends You Titles to Watch Actually Works." *Business Insider*, February 26, 2016. http://www.businessinsider.com/how-the -netflix-recommendation-algorithm-works-2016-2.

Saujani, Reshma. *Girls Who Code: Learn to Code and Change the World.* New York, NY: Viking, Penguin Young Readers Group, 2017.

Schwartz, Ariel. "Visualizing the Explosive Growth of the Robotics Industry." *Fast Company*, October 29, 2014. https://www.fastcompany.com/3037541 /visualizing-the-explosive-growth-of-the-robotics -industry.

Stack, Caroline. Showrunner's assistant, postproduction coordinator for FOX television. Phone interview. January 8, 2017.

Statista. "Number of Netflix Streaming Subscribers Worldwide from 3rd Quarter 2011 to 4th Quarter

2017 (in Millions)." Retrieved on March 1, 2018.
https://www.statista.com/statistics/250934
/quarterly-number-of-netflix-streaming-subscribers
-worldwide.

Statista. "Virtual Reality Software and Hardware
Market Size Worldwide from 2016 to 2020 (in
billion U.S. dollars)."Retrieved on February 28,
2018. https://www.statista.com/statistics
/528779/virtual-reality-market-size-worldwide.

Stiffler, Sara. Administrator for Warner Brothers. Phone
interview. February 28, 2018.

Telegraph. "The Evolution of the Mobile Phone: In
Pictures." Retrieved February 7, 2018. http://www
.telegraph.co.uk/technology/mobile-phones
/11339603/The-evolution-of-the-mobile-phone
-in-pictures.html.

US Department of Commerce, International Trade
Administration. "2016 Top Markets Report: ITA
Media and Entertainment." October 2016, https://
www.trade.gov/topmarkets/pdf/Media_and
_Entertainment_Top_Markets_Report.pdf.

ABOUT THE AUTHOR

Xina M. Uhl has written numerous educational books for young people. She has tackled subjects including history, biographies, technology, and health concerns. As the writer of a screenplay that features a group of young adults time-traveling on an ATV, she hopes to see her own film on the big screen one day. Visit her blog for details about her travels, publications, history tidbits, and the occasional cat picture.

PHOTO CREDITS

Cover Gorodenkoff/Shutterstock.com; back cover, pp. 4–5 (background) and interior pages nampix/Shutterstock.com; p. 5 PhilipImage/Shutterstock.com; pp. 7, 17, 28, 38, 47, 58 nampix/Shutterstock.com; p. 8 Interim Archives /Archive Photos/Getty Images; p. 11 Mark Nazh/Shutterstock. com; p. 12 martin-dm/E+/Getty Images; p. 14 kr7ysztof /E+/Getty Images; p. 17 a katz/Shutterstock.com; p. 19 Bobby Bank/WireImage/Getty Images; p. 21 JohnnyGreig /E+/Getty Images; p. 23 Pascal Deloche/GODONG /Corbis Documentary/Getty Images; p. 29 Mila Basenko /Shutterstock.com; p. 31 Jyrgen Stein/Stock4B/Getty Images; p. 32 Norbert Millauer/DDP/Getty Images; p. 35 Pictorial Press Ltd/Alamy Stock Photo; p. 39 Pavel L Photo and Video/Shutterstock.com; p. 40 Video_Creative/Shutterstock .com; p. 41 NetPhotos3/Alamy Stock Photo; pp. 44–45 Moviestore collection/Alamy Stock Photo; p. 48 Timofey _123/Shutterstock.com; p. 50 AFP/Getty Images; p. 53 seksan Mongkhonkhamsao/Moment/Getty Images; p. 56 Tinxi/Shutterstock.com; p. 59 Rawpixel.com/Shutterstock .com; p. 60 I am Nikom/Shutterstock.com; p. 63 sitthiphong /Shutterstock.com; interior design graphic (abstract circuit) Titima Ongkantong/Shutterstock.com.

Design: Michael Moy; Layout: Nicole Russo-Duca; Photo Researcher: Karen Huang